Train Up A Child
by Woodrow "Woody" Dingle

Train Up A Child

Copyright © 2019 by Woodrow Dingle

All scripture quotations are public domain courtesy of Bible Gateway: www.biblegateway.com.

All rights reserved. No part of this book may be reproduced, stored in a retrieval system, or transmitted in any form or by any means, electronic, mechanical, photocopying or otherwise without prior written permission from the author.

ISBN: 978-1-7339413-4-1

Edited by Latricia C. Bailey of LCB Enterprises

The Vision to Fruition Publishing House

www.vision-fruition.com

ALL RIGHTS RESERVED

PRINTED IN THE U.S.A.

Train Up A Child
In Loving Memory

WOODROW & BESSIE DINGLE
(Deceased Parents)

WILL & LUEVENIA DAVIS
(Deceased Grandparents)

By Woodrow Dingle

Dedications

First, I give honor to the Lord Jesus Christ, the one that brought me into this full life.

I dedicate this book to my beautiful wife, friend, lover, woman of God, my best thing for 18 years now, Jean Dingle.

To my lovely stepdaughter, Cherrie Hall; and my lovely seven children: Woodie Herring, II, Vernita Hinton, Lametrice Herring, Beatrice Hinton, Damien Herring, Crystal Thomas, and Lonnie Herring; and my sisters: Dorothy Perry and Sallie Squirewell.

To my Apostles, Tony and Cynthia Brazelton, Minister Jean and I love you both dearly. We give God praise and thank Him daily for bringing you into our lives and taking us down the pathway to help us grow and develop into who we are in Christ. Thank you for continuing to encourage us to believe, keep the faith, and continue trusting God in everything we do towards Him. To God be the glory for sending Jean and I all the way from Raleigh, N.C. to Maryland, to be fed the truth in the Word of God under a powerful, anointed man and woman of God who love God, His people, and who are sold out to God. They walk in the ways of God, fear Him in a way that they cannot sin against Him. They teach His words with boldness. Jean and I praise God all the time for a spiritual dad and mom like Apostles Tony and Cynthia Brazelton. They are the best apostles in the whole wide world.

To Elders Robert and Laneta Banks, we praise God for connecting you two with Jean and I in fellowship. You have helped us to grow and develop into who He has chosen us to be before the foundation of the world through the life of His son, Jesus the Christ. We thank both of you for being such a good gift from God to Jean and me. You both were very inspiring to us, compassionate, loving, and motivating. We thank you both so dearly, and give a special thanks to you, Elder Bobby, for encouraging me to do this book.

To Elder Gloria Corbett, thank you.

To Mike and Tonya Overton, Certified Coaches, thank you.

By Woodrow Dingle

Acknowledgements

John & Min. Truletta Hartsfield

Fred & Min. Helen Lewis

Deacon Charles & Gwen Williams

Pastor Greg & Karen Vinson

Elder Roscoe & Linda Johnson

Deacon Curtis and Shirley Leonard

Table of Contents

Training #1: 9
It Takes Discipline and Prayer 9
   ~ True Testimony One ~ 10
Training #2: 15
Racism and Raised to Forgive 15
   ~ True Testimony Two ~ 16
   ~ True Testimony Three ~ 18
Training #3: 23
Honor Thy Mother and Father, and Obey Grandma 23
   ~ True Testimony Four ~ 24
   ~ True Testimony Five ~ 26
Training #4: 31
Basic Training and Backsliding 31
   ~ True Testimony Six ~ 32
Training #5: 39
Marriage, Money, and Mindset 39
   ~ True Testimony Seven ~ 42
   ~ True Testimony Eight ~ 44
Training #6: 47
True Love and Marriage 47
   ~ True Testimony Nine ~ 48
Training #7: 52
Ministering and God's Gifts 52
   ~ True Testimony Ten ~ 54

Training #8:	62
Honoring the Shepherd	62
Training #9:	66
Ministry, Missions, and End Time Faith	66
The End Times	75
Fellowship	76
Honest	76
About the Author	81
About the Publisher	82

Training #1:
It Takes Discipline and Prayer

"Don't fail to discipline your children. They won't die if you spank them." Proverbs 23:13 NLT

By Woodrow Dingle

~ True Testimony One ~

It takes discipline and prayer to raise children, especially in these times. The Bible tells us in *Proverbs 13:24 NLT*:
"Those who spare the rod of discipline hate their children. Those who love their children care enough to discipline them.

I'm a living witness to this scripture verse. My upbringing centered around a very disciplined home. My two sisters and I were raised in a house with our Grandparents and their seven children. There were ten of us children in total. We attended all-black schools that were not integrated at that time. Life was so much easier then because people were more willing to discipline disobedient children. Teachers would discipline, neighbors would discipline, parents would discipline, and grandparents would all discipline disobedient children without question. With that type of discipline happening throughout communities, there was less of a need for corporal punishment.

Train Up A Child

My Grandpa and Grandma raised my two sisters and me on a farm with White people that owned the land as sharecroppers. My Grandpa and Grandma were provided with credit for seed, farming tools, living quarters, and food. They toiled the land and received an agreed share of the value of the crops with minor wages, as slaves. By the time I got to know my Grandpa he was disabled and unable to help my Grandma do much as far as the household chores went. It was as if I had to replace my Grandpa by helping my Grandma take care of the demands of the household and land. I took over my Grandpa's errands and workload. I was the one that would go to the shareowner to borrow his mule and wagon. I would then take the mule and hitch him to a wagon, go pick up my Grandma, take her to the grocery store, and bring her back home when she was done. Then, I would return the mule and wagon to the shareowner, disconnect the mule from the wagon, and put him in the pasture for grazing. This became a routine for me, and helped my Grandma and Grandpa take care of our home.

On Sunday mornings, my Grandma would make everybody in the house get up and walk to church, about four miles. We would get there, stay in church all day, then we had to walk back home afterwards. This was an eight-mile journey every week just for worship service. My Grandpa could not walk that far, so he would stay home. Someone always had to be home with him. It would cause some confusion every Sunday determining who would be the one to stay home with him. My Grandpa was sick, but not bedridden. He could get up, move around and walk inside and outside the house. He just couldn't walk far enough to attend church. My Grandma knew Grandpa didn't have a relationship with the Lord Jesus Christ, so she started having prayer meetings in our home every Tuesday night.

One Tuesday night shortly after we started having the prayer meetings in the home, I think everybody in the house except my Grandpa rededicated their lives back to Jesus. Grandpa had to accept Jesus as his Lord and Savior first by receiving the gift of Salvation. A year later, I saw how my Grandpa cried out to God and decided to give his life to Christ and ask for forgiveness for all his wrongdoing and sinful nature. That was the first time I had ever seen my Grandma so happy! She was rejoicing, dancing, and praising God like never before! One reason, I think, was because she was so glad that God put it in her heart to start having prayer meetings in her home. The second reason, I believe, was that if she had not had prayer meeting going on in her home, her husband would not have gotten to know Jesus Christ as his Savior and Lord. It wasn't long after this that my Grandpa passed away and went home to be with the Lord. I believe that my Grandma was able to have peace of mind when Grandpa died because she believed he was now with the Lord Jesus the Christ.

My Grandma continue having prayer meetings in our home. She opened our home up to the neighborhood and throughout the community. Whenever my Grandma heard about people in the neighborhood being sick, she would visit them. She would walk one to two miles to the neighbors' houses, and when she arrived, my Grandma would offer to pray for the family members and all those inside who needed prayer. They would always say, "Yes" to her offer. My Grandma really loved people and always reached out to help them.

By Woodrow Dingle

Training #2:
Racism and Raised to Forgive

"I'm not asking you to take them out of the world, but to keep them safe from the evil one." John 17:15 NLT

By Woodrow Dingle

~ True Testimony Two ~

My Grandma and I had just gotten off the Trailways Bus at the terminal. We were walking back home from the bus stop talking to one another and having a great conversation with each other. We were walking along the highway, and as we began to start down this hill, we noticed there was a tobacco barn off the left side of the highway about 50 feet at the bottom of the hill. Suddenly, a car pulled up beside me and my grandma. A black man driving the car asked my grandma and me if we would you like a ride. We said, *"Yes!"* and got in the car. As soon as the car started moving, about four, White racist Klansmen ran out from behind that tobacco barn waving large sticks in their hands, telling my Grandma and me that we had better be glad we caught a ride! Wow! What an awesome God we serve! He is a merciful God, a gracious God, a loving God, oh yes! He protected us from the Ku Klux Klan that was around and were well-known for what they stood for back in those days. Their terror of racist attacks was widely executed against Black people. When I was growing up, they would hang a Black person for nothing but the color of their skin. I could see them burning crosses while wearing white hoods over their faces. They would pass by our house and throw bricks, beer cans and bottles on our porch. Black people could not walk along the highway late at night alone, because the Klansmen would snatch them up and take them where no one would be able to find them. There have been many times I was walking along the highway at night alone. I could hear the noise of a car coming, and before I would see the headlights, I would hear the voice of God warning me and telling me to get over in the ditch and lay flat down on my stomach with my face down to the ground. God always reminds us that He is our protector no matter what the situation may be.

"He guards the paths of the just and protects those who are faithful to him." Proverbs 2:8 NLT

"Wise choices will watch over you. Understanding will keep you safe." Proverbs 2:11 NLT

As I grew up, I began to get a better understanding of what life was really like for Blacks while working on the farm with White folks. I would see how the White people would use my Grandpa and my Grandma and the whole family by getting over on all of us working on the farm with them as sharecroppers. Everything we would make they would take away and then just use us as their slaves. Grandma would walk to their house, clean, iron, wash their filthy clothes, clean their dirty dishes, and take out their nasty trash. Grandma would do all that work for them, but to them she was just a "nigger" and a slave. I would get so angry when I heard them call her that. I would say,

"*Grandma, why don't you say something to them?*"

She would just say to me, "*It's all right Woody Thomas.*"

~ True Testimony Three ~

One Tuesday afternoon, we were having our prayer meeting in our home. One of my friends, my neighbor, came by and asked me if I wanted to ride with him and his girlfriend to the laundromat to wash some clothes. I was only 14 years old, but I left without asking my Grandma for permission. We left, then we stopped at this little old country store because my friend wanted some wine to drink. He did not have enough money to buy it himself, so he asked his girlfriend for some money to help pay for the wine that he wanted. She would not give him any money to help buy the wine, so he got mad with her, and left the store. He got in the car and while spinning the tires on the car, drove down a pitch black, dark highway, speeding around 80 miles-per-hour! I was in the backseat of this yellow and white 1952 Bel Air Chevrolet with no seatbelt. The more his girlfriend and I would tell him to slow down before he hurt or killed somebody, the faster he would go, getting up to 110 miles per-hour! The next thing I saw was a red dirt, clay hill. At that point I found myself crawling up out of a ditch, holding my head looking for him. Then I heard him, and we started looking for his girlfriend, who we heard groaning and moaning in pain while lying in a ditch and moaning because she got hurt the worse. She got her neck broken. She didn't die from the car accident, instead she was physically disabled and could not turn her neck without turning her body. The driver and I were really blessed by the love and grace of God. We both came out of that horrible accident with just minor scratches. The car was said to have been going 116 miles per-hour, had turned over two or three times, and then landed in the middle of the highway. The three of us had been thrown out of the car into a ditch. The state trooper that found us thought that all of us were dead. We should have been, but for the grace of God! The enemy had tried to kill us, but God had another plan for us.

". . . But the son of God came to destroy the work of the devil. 1 John 3:8 NLT

"So now we can tell who are children of God and who are children of the devil." 1 John 3:10 NLT

It was my wife, Jean Dingle, whose aunt was in the car with me at the time of that car accident when I was younger. True story.

So, when I got back home to my Grandma's house, she said to me,

"Woody Thomas you should have been here in prayer meeting, I thought you was in the house. I was not aware

you had left out of the house. God said to me to tell you and your neighbor friends that you all are running and going too much. You need to slow down and stop running so much."

The next day God said to me,

"I want you to go and tell your neighbors what my servant said to you."

So, I went to my neighbor's house and told them what my Grandma had said to me about running and going so much, and that we need to slow down and stop running so much. So, when I told them what God had said for me to tell them, the one that had been driving the car that turned us over started laughing and making fun of me. He said to me,

"Your Grandma told you that, not me. So, you can stop. I am going to do what I want to do."

So, I said, *"Okay."* and left.

I didn't want to disobey my Grandma. There were times when I would get mad at my Grandma, go outside of the house and stay out there angry and mad. Then, later that night, I would come in the house, walk past my Grandma and would not say anything to her. I would just go upstairs to bed mad like that. When I would try to go to sleep, it seemed as if I was falling into a dark black pit that looked like Hell. I started yelling, crying, and running back down the stairs to my Grandma, and telling her I was sorry and beg her to please forgive me for being mad at her. Then she would say to me,

"I was waiting for that."

I had to honor my Grandma. I had to respect my Grandma. I had to love my Grandma. It was no other way around those words with my Grandma, God's servant. I had done as God lead me to do with my neighbor, eventhough he did not listen to me and instead he laughed at me, then spoke words against me, I just smiled and came back home. Three weeks after that conversation, his uncle killed him and his friends in a car accident. Thank God I listened to God's voice and obeyed Him.

Training #3:
Honor Thy Mother and Father, and Obey Grandma

"Children obey your parents because you belong to the Lord, for this is the right thing to do. 'Honor your father and mother.' This is the first commandment with a promise: If you honor your father and mother, 'things will go well for you, and you will have a long life on the earth." Ephesians 6:1-3 NLT

By Woodrow Dingle

~ True Testimony Four ~

My Grandma explained to me what had happened to my father and mother. She said if she would have had the money, she would have paid my mother to leave town and go somewhere else and not marry my father, because he did not "mean her any good at all." She saw the way he treated her, how he talked to her, and how jealous he was over her. So, when my mother got ready to marry my father, my Grandma told her not to marry that man, because he did not mean her any good. My mother questioned why she couldn't marry just like my Grandma did, so she went on and got married anyway. She married my father and he killed her, then he went to prison.

Grandma said he wanted his side of the family to raise me up, and her side of the family to raise my sisters up. She told him she would never separate my sisters and me from one another. Instead, she had to go to court before a judge to adopt her grandchildren. She told the judge that if he let her raise her grandchildren, she promised that they would never go without anything to eat. If she had a piece of bread to eat, they would have something to eat. So, the judge decided to let her take us all and raise us up together.

My Grandma wanted to know why my father took her daughter's life, so she decided to take all of us to prison to see him, and to ask him why. Grandma told him that he had better take a good look at all his children because after that day, he would never get to see us again.

Even though my Grandma raised me up, it was a secret that she kept from me throughout my school years. She always called me Woody Thomas Davis. When I became 18 years old, my Grandma had to take me to be registered for the U. S. Army. They had to go by the name that was on my Birth Certificate, which was the same as my father's name, Woodrow Thomas Dingle. I could not understand why my Grandma let me go that many years without telling me why she did not want to call me by my birth name. I really believe it was because he took my mother's life, and never told her why he did. I think it could have been a way for her to have had a peaceful mindset, by not calling his name which was also my name. Anyway, I forgave my Grandma for not letting me know my real name until I turned 18 years old.

~ True Testimony Five ~

I have a sister that lives in Charlotte, N.C. She has four daughters, one of which is a twin to the only son she has. I think I was around 34 years old at the time she called me and said her oldest daughter was in the hospital. They told my sister that they were going to transfer her daughter to a mental institution. I asked my sister what happened for them to send her to a mental institution. I heard the voice of God telling me to go, so I called my sister back and let her know I would be there that Friday between 12:00 and 1:30 p.m. It was late Thursday afternoon when she called me. That Friday morning, I caught the Trailways Bus to Charlotte, N.C. I got to Charlotte that afternoon around 12:30 p.m. My niece was there waiting for me at the bus terminal. On the way to the mental institution they were explaining to me what really happened.

When I got to the mental institution where she was, I first wanted to make sure she could talk and hear me clearly as to what the Lord had for me to say to her.

The first thing the Spirit of God did was to have me pray for her, then he led me in certain scriptures for her to confess after me speaking the word of God to her. I asked her if she really believed what she said out of her mouth as far as the word of God. She said, "Yes, I do Uncle Woody."

Then I asked her if she believed by faith that God could do a supernatural miracle in this situation and cause her to be home in three days, and she said *"Yes, I do Uncle Woody."*

I told her, *"God said if you believe that and take it by faith that it's already done, and you will be home by Monday afternoon."*

So, I repeated what the Spirit lead me to do Saturday and Sunday. I visited her Sunday, and I told her I would be leaving going back to Raleigh, N.C. after I left her in a few minutes. God told me to tell her,

By Woodrow Dingle

"It is finishing, and you will be home by Monday afternoon. All I want from you is a testimony, so call me Monday and give me that testimony."

She said, *"I will Uncle Woody."*

I left smiling in the love of God, and knowing that His grace, and mercy endure forever.

Sure enough, Monday afternoon my telephone rang and when I picked it up, it was my niece saying,

"Hi uncle Woody I am at home!"

When she said that we both started praising God, crying with joy because that was a supernatural miracle, God allowed to take place in her life in just three days. From then up until today she has never had that to happen to her again or even a complaint.

The people that did that to her were her friends. Instead they turned out to be her enemies. So, God lead me to go by their house and give them a visit before Michelle, my niece, took me over to their house. When I got there, I knocked on the door, they said to come in and so I walked in the house I spoke to everyone, then I let them know I was the uncle to the girl that they all did harm to. I let them know she was my niece, and God sent me there to let them know the wages of sin is death, the gift of God is eternal life through Jesus Christ our Lord. I was giving them a clear understanding of what it means to be in sin and to let them know God is not pleased with that at all. They said to me they were sorry, and asked if I would I forgive them, and they repented before me and God!

By Woodrow Dingle

Training #4:

Basic Training and Backsliding

"For the wages of sin is death, but the free gift of God is eternal life through Christ Jesus our Lord."
Romans 6:23 NLT

By Woodrow Dingle

~ True Testimony Six ~

I graduated from High School in June of 1967 and was drafted into the U. S. Army August 21, 1967. I had to go into the Army right after High School, so I did not have a summer vacation like my other classmates. Instead, I went to Fort Bragg, N. C. for my basic training.

I went back home for a week after my basic training, then was sent to Fort Dixie, N. J. where I was stationed for one year. Later, they sent me orders to go overseas to Vietnam, but before going, they sent me back home to Fort Dixie for another week. After that week was over, I left that Monday morning on my way to Vietnam. I knew then that it would be awhile, at least two years or more, before I would see my Grandma again. I don't know why, but I got angry at God for being away from my Grandma that length of time before seeing her again.

When I got to the company where we would be stationed which was HQ & Co. A 723D Maint BN, some of the other soldiers and I that were in the same company came together, and we had a party. Some of us got so drunk until we passed out. Even until this day I cannot tell you who carried me from the outside of my company in front of the building, took me in the building and laid me down on my bunk bed. From then on, I was backsliding from God.

I told God I would not turn back to Him until my time had come. I never had enough money to enjoy life like my neighbors and my running partner while coming up as a young man. I did not have a summer vacation to enjoy after graduation from High School. So, after going into the U. S. Army, then going overseas, whenever I got my paychecks, I would send them home to my Grandma for her to put them in the bank and save them for me until I got out of the Army.

While being in Vietnam, one day we came into the company for lunch. When we came in, we would always check our mail room first. This day we came in to check our mail room, then went to the mess hall to eat lunch. Five minutes after being in the mess hall for lunch, the Vietcong hit the mail room with a bomb! What if that would have taken place five minutes earlier? We all would had gotten killed! The grace, and the love of God lead us out early. I thank

God for his love, kindness, His mercy and goodness. When you are mad and upset, and backsliding, His love, His grace and mercy are still made available for you.

There were many times I was with my Grandma when she didn't have enough food to eat, didn't have enough clothes to put on our backs, shoes to put on our feet to wear, and how I would see her look up to heaven, with her arms around my neck praying, crying out to God, trusting God, believing God, waiting on God. I would see how God, would come through for my Grandma, blessing her with everything she trusted and believed him for, praise God. I know God is a good God, and the prayers of the righteous availeth much. I remembered how she prayed and asked God to make something out of her Grandson's life; make a great servant out of me; let me be used by God. Just look at me today being sold out for God and God only.

God blessed me to return home safely from Vietnam on April 15, 1970, but I still had not returned to Him. My Grandma and I went to the bank and withdrew all my money, and I gave my Grandma a large portion for saving it for me. Now, it was my time to enjoy life and I did. First thing I did was buy me a nice car, then I made myself a hot rod out of that car. It was known by everyone who would see it. They knew here comes Woody Davis with his bad ride, clean ride, pretty ride. First thing most folks wanted to know was where did I get all that money to fix up a car like that. My friends wanted to know, people in the neighborhood wanted to know, most families wanted to know, because they just could not believe what they were seeing. Most of them began to look at me like I had a lot of money, which was good because that's the way I carried myself.

When I was out enjoying life and having fun, I did not have a problem with ladies, because if I wanted one, I knew how to get her by chasing after her and pursuing her. I did everything in my willpower until I got her. There was a time coming up as a child when I was scared of little girls and growing up with them in the neighborhood, we all would be walking the highway together, and my sister's little friends would tell my sister they liked me and they wanted to kiss me. So, when I heard that, I would start running away! I remember my sisters would run and catch me, hold me down and let their friends kiss me. I would start crying and wiping my face off like it was nasty. The way my Grandma trained me up was by not beating me over my head with the word of God or teaching me the Word of God. It was just the way she lived her life, her lifestyle, her love, her compassion.

I saw the love she had for her husband when he was living, as well as when he was sick. She showed so much love for him until God called him home. My Grandma would tell me she is still married to him, and she did not want another man in her life. I am telling you my Grandma stayed her distance when a man came around her. I would tease my Grandma when a man got around her.

I would say, *"Grandma that man likes you."*

Grandma would say, *"That man has a wife, and I got a husband."*

I would say, *"Your husband is dead."*

Grandma would say, *"He's still my husband."*

I would say, *"Okay Grandma."*

As I became older in life, I noticed the fear that I would see in my Grandma's eyes when my uncle and I would start fussing with each other. When I took notice of this, I said to God,

"Please God, do not let me grow up in life with a death spirit on me or in me like that of my Father. Let her see that you can raise me up and not cause me to ever have a death spirit on me like that of my Father."

Sure enough, He raised me up and caused me not to have a death spirit nowhere near me or on me. Thank you, Father, you have been so good to me.

So, while backsliding from God out there in the world having fun and enjoying life, I fathered seven children out of wedlock. My time doing worldly things had to cease and I had to return to God, for the Bible says in,

Romans 6:23 NLT: "For the wages of sin is death but the free gift of God is eternal life through Christ Jesus our Lord."

John 10:10 KJBV: "the thief cometh not, but for to steal, and to kill, and to destroy . . ."

The seven children out of wedlock was a situation that God allowed me to stay in long enough until I understood that the things that I kept chasing so much became the things that would destroy my life. This was a situation that I had to believe and trust God to get me out of. I had to trust God with them and believe that He would draw all seven of them into the plans that He destined for their lives before the foundation of the world. I told God,

"If you bring me out of this one, for you I will live and never turn back."

He brought me out! Now, I live for Him! Yes, He is Lord of my life, and I am telling you that I never looked back. It's been forty years now, and I'm still running for my life. Praise God!

Training #5:
Marriage, Money, and Mindset

"Better to live on a corner of the roof than share a house with a quarrelsome wife." Proverbs 21:9 NIV

By Woodrow Dingle

In my first marriage I asked God should I marry this woman. God said to me, *"Do not marry her."*

Then, I heard another voice say, *"It's better to marry than to burn."*

I told myself I remember reading something in the Bible like that, so I went ahead and got married based on that Word. This was my first marriage and her second one. I had allowed the devil to convince me to get married. God did not tell me why He did not want me to get married, He just said don't do it.

We had only been in the marriage for about two years when my wife started saying that I was nothing to her. She told me that she knew when I was signing the paperwork for our house loan, she was not going to help me pay the mortgage on our house. I went to work one morning, and when I got back home, she had moved everything out of the house except for my bedroom set. She took everything else to the basement of her mother's house. I kept working, going to church, paying my tithes and offering, resting and sleeping well. Then, the next thing I know, she calls me and wants to come back. She came back home just until she got mad again, then she was gone again. She came back once more to ask me for divorce. I said to her, *"I am not going to give you a divorce you will have to get it yourself."*

After three years of marriage, God said to me, *"She never cared anything for you. All she wants is what you have."*

Oh my God! She had just said that to me two weeks prior! I told God that I was not blaming anybody but myself for this marriage. He told me not to get married, but I did it anyway. I know when God tells people to do something and they don't do it, then there are some consequences behind them disobeying and doing what He told them not to do. I was willing to suffer the consequences of my disobedience, but I didn't know how long I would suffer in this marriage, because now I had put myself in a position that I had to wait for God to bring me out of.

You see, God knew we all were going to make mistakes before He ever created and made us. All He wanted for you and me to do is just come to Him and be honest with him about whatever we did. Then we could repent and go forward living a holy and righteous life before the Lord and his people.

By Woodrow Dingle

Romans 8:28 *NLT* reminds us, *"And we know that God causes everything to work together for the good of those who love God and are called according to his purpose for them."*

~ True Testimony Seven ~

In my first marriage there came a time that I had to, trust God, depend on God, take every moment by faith and believe in God, because that was the tradition that my Grandma left for me follow.

My first wife got mad at me, jumped up and left me so often that it became a regular thing for her to do. So much so that I got used to her routine of leaving and returning home. My mortgage payment got behind, so every week when I got my paycheck, I would bring it home and put it with all my other checks that I had in my bedroom dresser draw. The next Friday that I brought my paycheck home, I opened the draw, I heard the voice of God say,

"Son, you will never catch your mortgage payment up like that. I want you to take all that money you have to my house and put it in the offering for tithes and offering."

When God said this to me, I did not have any other choice except to believe and trust God. My mortgage payment was already behind, and the bank loan officer was calling me threatening me about them foreclosing on the loan if I didn't produce that payment in a certain amount of days. My days were running out, so I could not do anything but to trust God with my whole bank account. I was 20 months of payments behind, which came to about $20,000 dollars. The first miracle was that God had my wife come back home long enough to get all the paperwork properly filled out and signed, so the house could be put on the market for sale. The second miracle was right after we finished the paperwork, I took the papers to my realtor, and she sold the house the next day. She got what was due to her, the loan got paid out, and I received a check for $3,000 dollars extra after the loan got paid off. I'm telling you God is good! You can't beat God giving, so just trust and believe in Him, have the faith.

God said to me, *"Son when I told you to give that money, I was not only thinking about your present, I was thinking towards your future. I saw how faithful you were towards me when I told you to give your all to me, and how you gave everything, so there will come a time that I am going to bless you with a larger house because of your belief and faith in me when you gave up that small house for me."*

~ True Testimony Eight ~

I am telling you my Father is faithful into His promises and will surely bring them to pass. My current wife, Jean, and I have been living in this large house God promised me for 15 years now. It is nothing like what we thought that we could ever afford right now. When Jean and I went looking for a house to live in, we were looking for a small rambler with everything on one floor. God reminded me of what He had said to me about the small house that I gave up for Him, when He told me to put my mortgage payment towards tithes and offering. He said this to me three days after we went looking for a house:

"Son you are looking too small. What I have for you is far bigger than what you are looking for."

There really came a time in my life that I wanted to know, *"Where have I come from?" "Where am I going?" "Why am I here?" "How can I know the truth?"* All these questions came before me. It was amazing that God blessed me with my first Bible. You know all those questions were in the back of that Bible, so when I saw this, it caused me to really fall in love with the word of God and get a clearer understanding of who I am, and the reason and purpose for me being here.

God said to me, *"It was I who destined your life before the foundation of the world. And even then I knew I was going to create you and bring you into life without your mother or father being involved in your life, because I wanted to be your whole life, your father, your mother, your sisters, and your brothers. I wanted to be your everything. I knew I had to put you with your grandma, which was my servant, so she could train you up in the way you should go, so when I started growing you up you would come up the way I want you to. Who would have said if your mother or father raised you that you would have had a life or relationship with me like you have now?*

I said to God, "I do not know, but if it took You to raise me up to have a life with You like I have and a relationship with You like I have, I thank You for raising me up and not ever causing me to see my mother or my father.

I am telling you, God is looking for some believers to come in agreement with Him and not get angry with Him when He shares the deep things in His heart towards you about your life, or start fussing at Him over what He is saying to you. I could have complained to God that everybody else had a mother and father involved in their life, why didn't You let me have a mother and father involved in mine? Or, I could have left God to go back sinning. You can run from Him or let Him bring you into His will that He has for your life, because what He promised to you. Just agree with what He said to you and give Him the thanks He is due.

"My child, listen to me and do as I say, and you will have a long good life." Proverbs 4:10 NLT

"Take hold of my instructions: don't let them go. Guard them, for they are the key to life." Proverbs 4:13 NLT

Training #6:
True Love and Marriage

"4 Love is patient, love is kind. It does not envy, it does not boast, it is not proud. 5 It does not dishonor others, it is not self-seeking, it is not easily angered, it keeps no record of wrongs. 6 Love does not delight in evil but rejoices with the truth. 7 It always protects, always trusts, always hopes, always perseveres."
1 Corinthians 13:4-7 NIV

By Woodrow Dingle

Jean and I grew up with one another in the farming industry. We lived not too far from one another, went to church together, and high school together. We were not high school sweethearts, just casual friends who talked and played around with each other. Back in those days, which was all we could do. I used to say to God, one day I want her to be my wife not realizing how powerful words are that come out of your mouth. Praise God. God knew. That was when Jean and I were teenagers. Look what happened, today we are husband and wife, and I can't do anything except smile and say look at God. He is good. I have many testimonies I can say that happened to me because of what I said out of my mouth and my Father God brought it to pass.

~ True Testimony Nine ~

God let my Grandma live to see five generations of her children's lives and to see five generations of her grandchildren's lives. Since then, her generation of grandchildren has grown to about eight generations.

I am the oldest male and my two sisters are the oldest females from this generation.

Grandma went home to be with the Lord on December 31, 2002, two years after Jean and I got married. She always said to me,

"Woody Thomas, I do not want to go home and be with the Lord until He blesses you with the wife that He wanted you to have."

So, again I knew Jean was the one. God told me when He brought me and Jean together that He would bless us with the life that Jesus gave that we might have. God has allowed me to see most of the promises that He promised me in singleness and in marriage. Praise God! Glory to God! He is a good God.

Jean had been staying in Maryland since we finished high school, and I was still in Raleigh, North Carolina, where we were both born and raised. When she came to Raleigh to visit her family during the holidays, the Lord brought us back together. Her sister would let me know when Jean would be coming home, and I would visit her. She had been married, but her husband got killed. I had been married and as I said earlier, my wife divorced me.

By Woodrow Dingle

So, after God brought Jean and I back together, she realized it was God's doing and not my doing. I told her God said she would be my wife and since she had a hard time believing me, the Holy Spirit would confirm it for her. He would let her know that this was God's doing and not mine. He said when it happens, she will go back to Upper Marlboro, MD. This will give me a testimony and let me know that I was telling her the truth. Sure enough, it happened just like I said to her. Then, sometime later I asked her would she marry me. She struggled with that proposal until she brought me before her pastors, Tony and Cynthia Brazelton of Victory Christian Ministries International. She called me and said she wanted me to meet her pastors before we could get married.

I packed some clothes and went to see her for the weekend. When we got to church, she took me into her pastor's office. I introduced myself to them, and they introduced themselves as being her pastors and were looking out for her well-being. I easily understood where they were coming from, so I began telling them how my grandparents would make us walk to church every Sunday morning and shared how we had weekly prayer meetings. As I was sharing with them, we were laughing, then suddenly Jean asked her pastors what God was saying to them about Woody. First, they looked over at her, then after a while, she asked again. They said, *"Sister Jean, do you really want to know what God was saying to us about him? He said that he really is a blessed man."* I should have asked her pastors at that time what God was saying to them about Jean, but that's all I am going to say about that.

Pastors Tony and Cynthia Brazelton joined Jean and I together in marriage on December 2, 2000, which will be 19 years together this year, 2019. It has been a blessing being married and sitting under the leadership of a man and woman of God who are sold out to God, fear God, love God hear from God, see like God sees, and love their flock like God loves the sheep. They wouldn't let one of their sheep go astray without going after it.

By Woodrow Dingle

Training #7:

Ministering and God's Gifts

"This is why I remind you to fan into the flames the spiritual gift God gave you when I laid my hands on you." 2 Timothy 1:6 NLT,

I have worked for about 48 years, so I knew whenever there was a door that God opened for me to have a job, I made sure when I got my paychecks that I gave God His portion before taxes came out. I also never had to use an alarm clock, or anything to wake me up, only the Spirit of God Himself. Since God had Jean and me to retire at the end of 2011, the Spirit of God still wakes me every morning, just like it did when I was working on those jobs at the exact same time every morning.

I remember there came a season in my life when God had me attend different churches. He would have me go to several churches for the same length of time, then attend another church for the same. So, finally I asked God what was going on? God told me it was so that I would understand the true gospel through the Word of God, from the false gospel through man's religious and self-made gospel.

God told me, *"Son, I heard my servant, your Grandma, pray many prayers for Me to make something out of your life. And I did make you a prophet within the five-fold ministries in my Word. The prayers of your grandma, availeth much."*

By Woodrow Dingle

"The earnest prayer of a righteous person has great power and produces wonderful results." James 5:16 NLT

~ True Testimony Ten ~

I came from Vietnam in April 15, 1970, when I received my honorable discharge from the U.S. Army. Now here it is today, and I can still wear my same uniform as though I just got out of the U.S. Army. I have been out of the U.S. Army now for 49 years. If that's not supernatural then I do not know what is. I am 72 years of age right today and I do not know what a headache is less any other sickness and disease.

"Don't be misled, you cannot mock the justice of God. You will always harvest what you plant." Galatians 6:7 NLT

I will never ever forget, I remember laying in my bed one night, I do not know when my Spirit left out of my body, but I remember being in heaven with God. I did not see Him, yet I remember Him talking to me. It was like when He spoke to Moses on the backside of the mountain when God gave him the Ten

Commandments. It was so peaceful, I knew I was in His presence, His love, His glory, and I really did not want to leave, so I said to God,

"Let me stay here with you. I do not want to go back."

He told me that it was not my time yet. He was sending me back for me to let His people know of His return. No man knows the minute nor the hour of God's return. He wanted me to let them know the season and the time of His return. The next thing I knew my eyes were open, and I began to see my Spirit enter back into my body like a shadow formed in my image. God also told me what ministry I was to minister out of from the five-fold ministry.

"Whatever is good and perfect comes down to us from God our Father, who created all the lights in the heavens. He never changes or casts a shifting shadow." James 1:17 NLT

"This is why I remind you to fan into flames the spiritual gift God gave you when I laid my hands on you." 2 Timothy 1:6 NLT

"Giving a gift can open doors: it gives access to important people!" Proverbs 18:16 NLT

By Woodrow Dingle

God told me the ministries that He is leading me into are ministries that are going to rise unlike ever before in the end times and last days right before His return. He said it is the time and season, for His return. I'm telling you right now, the Lord Jesus Christ is on his way back.

"For I know the plans I have for you," says the Lord. "They are plans for good and not for disaster to give you a future and a hope." Jeremiah 29:11 NLT

"Tune your ears to wisdom and concentrate on understanding." Proverbs 2:2 NLT

God said to me to tell his people that He created me, called me, and chose me, before the foundation of the world. God sent His Son to trade my life for his to conform me into the image of his Son, Jesus Christ, as a living example of him living here on earth. He told me to let His people know what my son did through his death, burial, and resurrection on the cross.

"Don't be misled; remember that you can't ignore God and get away with it: a man will always reap just the kind of crop he sows." Galatians 6:7 NLT

"O Sovereign LORD, you have only begun to show your greatness and the strength of your hand to me, your servant. Is there any god in heaven or on earth who can perform such great and mighty deeds as you do? Deuteronomy 3:24 NLT

"And we know that the son of God has come, and he has given us understanding so that we can know the true God. And now we live in fellowship with the true God because we live in fellowship with his son, Jesus Christ. He is the only true God, and he is eternal life." 1 John 5:20 NLT

"Dear children, keep away from anything that might take God's place in your heart." 1 John 5:21 NLT

"So all of us who have had that veil removed can see and reflect the glory of the Lord. And the Lord who is the Spirit makes us more and more like him as we are changed into his glorious image." 2 Corinthians 3:18 NLT

"I am the Lord, and I do not change. That is why you descendant of Jacob are not already destroyed." Malachi 3:6 NLT

God said, *"The reason that you can still fit in your U.S. Army uniform and can still wear it after 49 years, is because I'm not a changing God, and my son can't change. The same way with your health, it is finished, every stripe that was taken upon that cross was for your healing transgression. By his stripes you were healed.*

Through the death, burial, and resurrection of His son Jesus Christ God gave us everything we need to go and replenish the earth. He made you and his son, Jesus.

"For God knew his people in advance and he chose them to become like his son, so that his son would be the first born among many brothers and sisters." Romans 8:29 NLT

"Dear friends, we are already God's children, but he has not yet shown us what we will be like when Christ appears But we do know that we will be like him, for we will see him as he really is" 1 John 3:2 NLT

"And all who have this eager expectation will keep themselves pure, just as he is pure." 1 John 3:3 NLT

"For every child of God defeats this evil world, and we achieve this victory through our faith." 1 John 5:4 NLT

"And who can win this battle against the world? Only those who believe that Jesus is the son of God." 1 John 5:5 NLT

"And Jesus Christ was revealed as God's Son by his baptism in water and by shedding his blood on the cross[b]—not by water only, but by water and blood. And

the Spirit, who is truth, confirms it with his testimony. 7 So we have these three witnesses[c]— 8 the Spirit, the water, and the blood—and all three agree. 9 Since we believe human testimony, surely we can believe the greater testimony that comes from God. And God has testified about his Son. 10 All who believe in the Son of God know in their hearts that this testimony is true. Those who don't believe this are actually calling God a liar because they don't believe what God has testified about his Son." 1 John 5:6-10 NLT

So, in every believer God put his Holy Spirit on the inside of each one of us, so the Spirit would lead and guide us into all truth. What is truth? His words are truth. When you become born again you now have a new spirit living on the inside of you. Your new spirit and the Holy Spirit must become one united with each other? Then you let the Spirit lead you into the Word of God. You see through the finished death of His son Jesus on that cross, God gave all the believers a goal in life and gave us everything we need to go replenish and dominate the earth.

We do not have to be sidetracked by an unending search for truth. God's goal for us is to make us like Christ. Are you willing to change yourself to know

Christ better? Will you change some of your plans, goals, and desires to conform with what you learn about Christ? Whatever you must change or give up, having Christ and becoming one with him will be more than worth the sacrifice.

Philippians 3:9-10 NLT says, "9 and become one with him. I no longer count on my own righteousness through obeying the law; rather, I become righteous through faith in Christ.[a] For God's way of making us right with himself depends on faith.10 I want to know Christ and experience the mighty power that raised him from the dead. I want to suffer with him, sharing in his death,"

I was like Apostle Paul. I gave up everything, family, friendship, and freedom to know Christ and His resurrection power, but I must make sacrifices to enjoy it to the highest or fullest degree. I said that I wanted to know Christ, to be like Christ, and to be all Christ had in mind for me. This goal took all of Paul's energy.

Before I got out of high school, I did make a choice to go into the U.S. Army. After that, I didn't make a choice to be or to do anything else in life until I went to see the movie, *The Passion of the Christ*. It was then when I began to focus on myself thinking, why was this man was going through all that he was going through for a little person like me? I didn't even feel worthy at that time, for this man to be going through all that on a cross just for me. Now my whole mind, heart, and soul, got to find out from this man why he did all that on the cross for me, and why he loves me so much that he decided to go through all that suffering on the cross.

By Woodrow Dingle

Training #8:

Honoring the Shepherd

"And God has places in the church first of all prophets, second of all apostles, third teachers, then miracles, then gifts of healing, of helping, of guidance, and of different kinds of tongues." 1 Corinthians 12:28 NIV

Apostle Tony and Cynthia Brazelton, I have loved you both from the first time I met you. I knew you were real men and women of God. Your teaching of the truth in the Word of God has caused me to keep the faith and continue to believe and trust God throughout my life. Many times, while sitting under your teaching I personally heard conversations that God and I had before I ever got to know both you. When I asked God about this, He told me that it was confirmation coming from Him to let me know that I was in His will and doing His will.

Apostle Tony and Cynthia, Jean and I have been faithfully involved in ministry ever since we have been to Victory Christian. We work in various ministries here, because we understand that service is about God, and we came to be servants. God told me in 2011 that the mission field that I had been sent on was over with, and He wanted me to take that time to give Him my full-time service in the Spirit realm.

"Don't put your confidence in powerful people; there is no help for you there." **Psalm 146:3 NLT**

My Father taught me, *"Take my words to heart. Follow my commands, and you will live. Proverbs 4:4 NLT*

By Woodrow Dingle

"A mocker seeks wisdom and never finds it, but knowledge comes easily to those with understanding." Proverbs 14:6 NLT

"Getting wisdom is the wisest thing you can do! And whatever else you do, develop good judgment." Proverbs 4:7 NLT

We both retired at the end of 2011 as God instructed us to do. We've been sold out for God, only working and serving like the Holy Spirit leads us to do. We have received blessings on top of blessings. To God be the glory.

"Pray like this: Our Father in heaven, may your name be kept holy. May your Kingdom come soon. May your will be done on earth as it is in heaven." Matthew 6:9-10 NLT

"Seek the Kingdom of God above all else, and live righteously and he will give you everything you need." Matthew 6:33 NLT

Train Up A Child

By Woodrow Dingle

Training #9:
Ministry, Missions, and End Time Faith

"And so, dear brothers and sisters who belong to God and are partners with those called to heaven, think carefully about this Jesus whom we declare to be God's messenger and High Priest." Hebrews 3:1 NLT

I made a choice in my life to pursue the goal that God gave me through the death, burial, and the resurrection of the cross. I pursued, and I chased. I did not let my friends, stop me. I did not let my family stop me. I did not let my seven children stop me. I did not let friendship stop me. I did not let my money stop me, and I did not let world system, nor the world affairs stop me from finding out who Jesus Christ was and what his life was all about in my life.

By me doing that, I made him to be priority over my entire life. God said to me, *"Son I am well pleased in you, because you have made me the goal of your life."*

I said to God, *"What do you mean, I made you the goal of my life."*

God replied, *"Son, this is in the spirit. Let me give you a clear understanding in the natural."*

He gave me this example of Michael Jordan grown up:

> *After he got grown he decide to make a choice in his life, that he wanted to be a professional basketball player, so he made that choice, then he pursued it, he chased after it, he did not let anything nor anyone stop him from running*

after the choice he made. Now look at him today. He achieved the goal of his life as a professional basketball player. It was the same way with you, son, when you pursued and chased after what my son did for you on that cross, and you did not let anybody stop you, it brought you into why I made you my before the foundation of the world. That's who you are my son, that's the goal of your life my son, that's who you are.

Hebrews 4:12 NLT **reminds us:**
"For the word of God is alive and powerful. It is sharper than the sharpest two-edged sword, cutting between soul and spirit, between joint and marrow. It exposes our inner most thoughts and desires."

When you let the Holy Spirit lead you into the Word, then give you what scripture to study, and whatever is going on in your heart that is not of God, the Spirit of God will do surgery in your heart and soul, then he will put his words there.

"I have hidden your word in my heart, that I might not sin against you." Psalm 119:11 NLT

"And so, dear brothers and sisters who belong to God and are partners with those called to heaven, think carefully

about this Jesus whom we declare to be God's messenger and High Priest." Hebrews 3:1 NLT

"My dear children, I am writing this to you so that you will not sin. But if anyone does sin, we have an advocate who pleads our case before the Father. He is Jesus Christ, the one who is truly righteous." 1 John 2:1 NLT

To *"seek the kingdom of God above all else"* according to *Matthew 6:33 NLT,* means to put God first in your life, to fill your thoughts with his desires, to take his character for your pattern and to serve and obey him in everything."

"Seek the Kingdom of God above all else . . ." God is saying through the death, burial and resurrection of the cross in what my son Jesus Christ did before the foundation of the world, I gave my people a goal in this life and that was making them my son. The only thing I'm saying is before they go about life doing anything else, find out why I created them and made them in the image of my son, Jesus. And when they find that out first above all else and live a righteous life. And he will give you everything you need.

Our goal should be Christ. Yet how do we know him better?

(1) Study the life of Christ in the Gospels. See how Christ lived and responded to people. See Matthew 11:29 *NLT*.

(2) Study all the New Testament references to Christ. See Colossians 1:15 *NLT*.

(3) As you worship and pray, let the Holy Spirit remind you of Christ's words. See John 14:26 *NLT*.

(4) Take up Christ's mission to preach the Gospel and learn from his sufferings. See Matthew 28:19 *NLT* and Philippians 3:10 *NLT*.

We carry the Kingdom of God on the inside of us, and we are called to release it to the world; our families, our communities, our cities, and the nations. What starts in the local churches was never meant to stay in the confines of its four walls. Kingdom movement is evidenced through believers using their gifts to meet tangible needs.

Our worst day doesn't define who He says we are. God is quick to remind us of his great love for us. He revives. God manifests His transforming presence where hearts are unified in the pursuit of Him and where His presence is, the Kingdom is released to transform lives. The call of every believer is to live naturally supernaturally with the ministry of Christ as their example.

He's with me even as I write, yet it still requires me to be fully present. As artists and creatives, our greatest challenge may be facing the fear of being misunderstood or misinterpreted. It'll always feel like a big deal to give away something so deeply connected to our hearts and our souls, knowing that God is the only one who will ever completely understand it and fully appreciate it.

God is at work transforming us into His image, His seed, His DNA, His genetic code lies within us, (uniform for the forms of life) and everything inside of us is being conformed to the image of love.

"Those who have been born into God's family do not make a practice of sinning because God's life is in them. So, they can't keep on sinning because they are children of God." 1 John 3:9 NLT

When God took up residence in your heart when you were born again, He elevated your spirit to its rightful position. You were created to rule over all of God's done with your hands (handiwork) you have been crowned with His glory and majesty; (glory) worshipful praise, honor, and thanksgiving, giving thanks to God.

(Majesty) sovereign power, greatness, or splendor of quality or character. Your Spirit was made to rule over all things, and that includes your own soul (soulish) realm more at regimen, Kingdom.

"Yet you made them only a little lower than God and crowned them* with glory and honor." Psalms 8:5-6 NLT*

"You gave them charge of everything you made, putting all things under their authority." Psalms 8:6 NLT

I remember when my Grandma, was training me up in the way I should go, and she could not read, because she said that she did not get any further than the sixth grade. I remember going over some words with her trying to help her read. I began to see how she started to believe and began to trust that the Holy Spirit on the inside of her taught her how to read not just words, but also the Word of God. Despite her limited reading, the fact that she became the assistant pastor of her church was amazing. I'm telling you my God is good, my father, my daddy my everything!

God gave you and me a goal in this life even before He created the foundation of the world, and the goal that He gave to us was that He made you and me His son. We can now strengthen the brethren and as witnesses declare with boldness, *". . .because as He is, so are we in this world."* 1 John 4:17 AMP

For this reason, we have the freedom to make the choice or not as to whether we want to have Jesus as our lord and savior or not. Why would God place a tree in the garden and then command Adam to eat from it? God wanted Adam to obey, but God gave Adam the freedom to choose. Without choice, Adam would have been like a prisoner, and his being would have been false.

The two trees represent choices we are given. When you are faced with making the choice, always choose to obey God. He gives us the choice of choosing life or death. When you choose life, you choose what His son, Jesus, did throughout the death, burial, and resurrection of the cross. When you choose death, you have chosen the worldly ways and its affairs.

These are the two choices that God has given us to live out in this life. God told me that He has many Christian believers that are not making the choice to be men or women of God, so they are no different from Adam. They are going about this Christian life as believers living as prisoners with a false pretense.

"Seek the Kingdom of God above all else, and live righteously, and he will give you everything you need." Matthew 6:33 NLT

What God is saying through the finished work in what my Son, Jesus, has already done on the cross for you and I was that he took on your life and gave you his life. By him giving you his life, he gave you and I everything we need to go and replenish the earth. By you being his child, he gave you a goal in this life. He is saying whatever you do within this life, find out first why He created you, and made you man or woman of God before you go about this life doing anything else.

God made you His son or daughter, and made you righteous, then put you on earth so you could discover that life first, and it will bring you into understanding who you are as men and women of God. You would discover how powerful and anointed you are on earth as in heaven.

The End Times

Jesus is on his way back. Yes, we are living in the end times and the last days. It is the season and the time of Christ to return. He is about to crack the sky.

"6 And you will hear of wars and threats of wars, but don't panic. Yes, these things must take place, but the end won't follow immediately. 7 Nation will go to war against nation, and kingdom against kingdom. There will be famines and earthquakes in many parts of the world. 8 But all this is only the first of the birth pains." Matthew 24:6-8 NLT

"I tell you the truth, this generation will not pass from the scene until all these things take place. Heaven and earth will disappear, but my words will never disappear." Matthew 24:34-35 NLT

I heard the voice of God say it's the season that *Romans 14:11 NLT* says, "As surely as I live,' says the Lord, 'every knee will bend to me, and every tongue will declare allegiance to God."

By Woodrow Dingle

Fellowship

"6 This confirms that what I told you about Christ is true. 7 Now you have every spiritual gift you need as you eagerly wait for the return of our Lord Jesus Christ. 8 He will keep you strong to the end so that you will be free from all blame on the day when our Lord Jesus Christ returns. 9 God will do this, for he is faithful to do what he says, and he has invited you into partnership with his Son, Jesus Christ our Lord. 1 Corinthians 1:6-9

"1 Is there any encouragement from belonging to Christ? Any comfort from his love? Any fellowship together in the Spirit? Are your hearts tender and compassionate? 2 Then make me truly happy by agreeing wholeheartedly with each other, loving one another, and working together with one mind and purpose." Philippians 2:1-2 NLT

"We proclaim to you what we ourselves have actually seen and heard so that you may have fellowship with us. And our fellowship is with the Father and with his Son Jesus Christ." 1 John 1:3 NLT

Honest

"And the seeds that fell on the good soil represent honest, good-hearted people who hear God's Word, cling to it, and patiently produce a huge harvest." Luke 8:15 NLT

Notes

By Woodrow Dingle

Notes

Notes

By Woodrow Dingle

Notes

About the Author

Prophet Woodrow "Woody" Dingle is a committed deacon leader, serving over about 39 other deacons, and working in the body of Christ with four other ministries at Victory Christian Ministries International. Prophet Woody has been serving in ministries for 18 years, since 2001, right after he and Jean got married. Prophet Woody loves the ministries and loves serving God's people, because he loves people and loves the Lord, Jesus Christ.

Born to the late Woodrow and Bessie Dingle in Wendell, N.C., Wake County, Prophet Woody graduated from James E. Shepard High School. He served three years in the U.S. Army, while stationed in Vietnam for 16 months. He has seven children, and he married his high school girlfriend, sweetheart, and lover, Jean, whose been his wife for 18 years now. She has been the best thing to happen to him. Glory to God!

Prophet Woody loves football, basketball, tennis, shooting pool, wrestling, car racing, ice skating, and exercising. He enjoys music, Tyler Perry movies, crime shows like CSI and Law & Order to name a few. More than anything else, he loves the Lord, who first loved him, yet when he was a sinner. He knows the reason and purpose God sent him here. He is faithful to God and His Word in Matthew 4:4 NLT:

"But Jesus told him, 'No!' The scriptures say, 'people do not live by bread alone, but by every word that comes from the mouth of God.'"

By Woodrow Dingle

About the Publisher

At **the Vision to Fruition Publishing House**, we are dedicated to helping others bring their personal, business, ministry & nonprofit visions to fruition.

Whether it's as grand as a book you want to write, a business you want to start, a conference or event you want to host, a ministry you want to launch or an organization you want to start; or as small as needing a computer repair, logo design or web design; **The Vision to Fruition Publishing House** is the publishing branch of **the Vision to Fruition Group**. We will help you walk through the process and set you up for success! At **the Vision to Fruition Group** we don't have clients, we have *Visionaries*. We provide solutions to equip others to pursue their visions and dreams with reckless abandon.

In 2018 we published twenty-three authors, eight of which were Amazon Bestsellers. We would love for you to join our family of Visionaries as well!

Learn more here: **www.vision-fruition.com**

www.ingramcontent.com/pod-product-compliance
Lightning Source LLC
Chambersburg PA
CBHW070518090426
42735CB00012B/2826